The #2022 Air Fryer Cookbook

Delicious and Easy-Going Recipes For Beginners and Advanced Users | Your Everyday Air Fryer Book

Marc Goodwin

ISBN - 9798760352873

Table of Contents

Marc Goodwin

Section One:
The Air Fryer – What is it and how do I use it?

Welcome to the wonderful world of air frying! If you're new to the game of air frying, and you're thinking about joining the ranks of people who've fallen in love with it then this section of the book is perfect for you. We'll take you through what the air fryer is, how it works and whether or not it'll be right for you.

If you've already bought an air fryer, don't worry! This book still has plenty of useful information for you, including a section below with some tips and tricks you may not know. If you want to get the most out of your air fryer, stick around. And then of course, we've also got a list of recipes curated for you, taking you all the way from breakfast to dessert (with some tasty snacks thrown in of course!) so you don't have to worry about going hungry.

What is an air fryer and how does it work?

So, first things first: what is an air fryer?

You might be wondering this very thing if you're new to the game. Air fryers have blown up quite a bit over the past couple of years, and despite being a relatively new invention (they've only been around since about 2010), they're set to become a staple in homes around the world.

Simply put, an air fryer is exactly what it sounds like – it's a small oven that fries food using air rather than large quantities of oil. They're as simple to use as a conventional oven – you put the food in, you set the temperature and you cook – but because of the cooking method, they tend to be a lot faster. None of the recipes you'll see in this book will take more than 20 minutes to cook in the air fryer.

The next important question you might be asking is: how does it work?

The idea of being able to have your favourite fried foods without having to deep fry them seems too good to be true, but it makes a lot of sense when you understand how the air fryer actually works. There's a lot of complicated science behind it, but we'll break it down into simple terms.

Technically, due to the fact that your food only requires a little oil you aren't actually frying it – you're roasting it. However, due to the method of cooking, the food tastes more like it's been fried than baked, making it the perfect way to make up healthier versions of your favourite comfort foods.

The air fryer cooks from the top down – there's a heating mechanism in the top, and a powerful little fan. Because the inside of the air fryer is a lot smaller than your conventional oven, the fan packs more of a punch when it comes to cooking your food. The extreme force of the hot air circulating all around your food helps to give it that nice crispy 'fried' effect, without all of the grease and oil that comes with conventional frying methods.

When they first came on the scene air fryers were notably expensive, and they were seen as the kitchen gadget that only the uber-rich lifestyle influencers could afford. As the years have gone by though, more air fryers have entered the market, and some of them are at a very affordable price point. If you're considering buying an air fryer and making your way into the world of healthy frying, there's never been a better time for it!

The pros and cons to using an air fryer

You might still be on the fence about whether or not an air fryer is right for you. Don't worry about it too much – we understand that it can be difficult to make a big purchase for your kitchen if you aren't completely sold on the idea yet. We also know that it can be hard to trawl through all of the information online to find out what you need, so we've done it for you! We've broken down the biggest reasons for and against buying an air fryer and brought them together for you here.

Pros to using an air fryer:

The pros of an air fryer are quite simple, because almost all of them revolve around the most important feature of the air fryer – you use less oil.

They're healthier than conventional deep or shallow frying

Air fryers by nature will use less oil than other methods of frying foods. There are a couple of benefits to using less oil in your foods, and the biggest of those is that it's better for your health. It's a well-known fact that foods high in oil can lead to heart disease, diabetes, the potential to have a stroke, and can contribute to obesity in the long run. It's a good idea to limit your intake of oil, and make sure the oil you do have is healthy – like olive oil.

Marc Goodwin

Less oil means less mess

Less oil in your cooking isn't just good for your heart – it's good for the home too! Cooking with oil is notoriously messy, and potentially even dangerous. Even with a splatter screen over your pots and pans, deep frying foods in your kitchen can still result in a thin film of oil all over your stove top, walls and appliances – if this isn't cleaned properly, it can increase your risk of having an oil fire in the long term.

Not only that, but when you deep fry foods, your whole house will smell like oil for a really long time. Now we all love the smell of fresh doughnuts while they're being cooked, but there's something called 'too much of a good thing'. Using less oil and cooking with an air fryer means you won't be living with the lingering smell of grease for days after you make your favourite fried snack.

Good for the family

We've briefly talked about safety above. Less oil reduces your risk of running headfirst into a grease fire. There's another reason you should consider the air fryer though, and that's the safety of your children. Many of us love cooking with our children – it's a great chance to bond with our little ones and instil a love of cooking in them. Unfortunately, when cooking with lots of oil it's often dangerous for little ones to be in the kitchen with you, in case they accidentally get hot oil on them. With an air fryer though, it's much safer for kids to be in the kitchen with you, making it perfect for families!

Cons to using an air fryer:

We'll admit, nothing is perfect – even the air fryer. We've made up a list of small issues you might have when it comes to buying an air fryer, and how to weigh these cons up with all of the benefits an air fryer will net you.

They are an investment

Air fryers can be a real investment, especially if you want a large one that can withstand a lot of cooking. The high-end air fryers can be upwards of $200/£120. Of course, if you're new to the world of air fryers there are some cheaper ones on the market too – some can cost you around £35/$50. Shop around for a nice budget one (or go in on a sale) if you're a beginner to the world of air frying.

They're quite small

Air fryers aren't as big as a conventional oven. This is actually something that can be a pro or a con! The small size of air fryers means that they'll be able to fit in almost any kitchen without causing you any problems. However, that small size can also be a bit of a hindrance. While some of the more expensive air fryers have a capacity of 12 litres, most of the ones you'll find on the market will be about 2-4. To get around this, we recommend cooking food in batches and keeping the excess food warm in the oven.

They do have their limitations

And lastly, there are a few foods that shouldn't really be cooked in the air fryer, and a few more that need extra care to be taken. We'll go through this in more detail below.

Marc Goodwin

Things you should avoid cooking in an air fryer

We're going to put our hands up now and admit, even though our air fryers can cook most things, they can't cook everything. There are some things that you should be cautious about cooking in your air fryer or avoid altogether. Don't worry, the list isn't that long!

Battered foods

Don't worry, don't worry! We aren't about to tell you to forgo the onion rings. You can cook battered foods in the air fryer, but you need to be careful how you do it. If you want to cook battered foods, we recommend freezing them first, to make sure that the batter solidifies. If the batter is still wet when it goes into the air fryer, it runs the risk of little bits coming off and getting into the machine. If you can switch out the batter for breadcrumbs, we recommend it!

Fresh greens and light, thinly sliced foods

Fresh, light foods don't do all that well in the air fryer, due to the cooking method. The force of the air that circulates in the machine tends to whip up light foods, and you'll end up with the same problem as fresh batter. If you do cook thinly sliced or light foods, we recommend pinning the food down using a toothpick.

Whole roasts

Speaking of density... Too much can be a bad thing. The problem with whole roasts of meat is that they're too dense. It's hard to get a whole roast of meat cook evenly, which is dangerous. While it might seem like your food is cooked (or even burned) on the outside, if you're cooking a particularly big roast, it might still be raw on the inside. If you're doing a whole roast, we recommend using an oven.

Cheese

Before you start panicking, don't worry! We're not telling you to steer clear of your beloved halloumi fries. Cheese is a great ingredient to add to any dish that you want to put in your air fryer, but just be wary of putting cheese directly into your air fryer. Because it has such a low melting point, it's all too easy for cheese to melt quickly or burn and slip through the gaps in the air fryer basket. If you want to avoid this, coat your cheese in something or use it as a topping, and line your basket.

Grains like pasta and rice

Rice and pasta both need to be cooked in water before anything else can be done with them. If you want to cook them in the air fryer – to make fried rice, for example – you'll need to cook them in water first, as per the instructions on the packet. Then you can add them to the air fryer.

Marc Goodwin

Tips to make the most out of your air fryer

Now, if you're set on the idea of getting an air fryer (as we honestly think most people should be), or even if you're someone who's already got an air fryer but wants to make the most out of it, this is the section that you'll find the most interesting. There are quite a few tips to really get the most out of your air fryer, so we've divided them up for you!

The oil issues

There are a few issues around oil that are important to mention. Here are some important things to bear in mind:

- The amount of oil you use is important

  - Remember that you're air frying, not deep frying. Be sparing with the oil you use, because adding too much oil can actually make your air fryer less effective. When you use oil, we recommend brushing it over the top of food or putting it into a spray bottle to limit the amount you use.

- Consider the type of oil you're using

  - We recommend using oil or butter rather than a non-stick cooking spray. It's quite common for cooking sprays (especially low-calorie cooking sprays) to have chemicals in them. These chemicals can eat away at the non-stick coating of your air fryer basket.

- Use an oil with a high smoke point. Your air fryer will cook at a high temperature, so you ideally want your oil to have a smoke point no lower than 200°C (400°F). Some examples of good oils to use in your air fryer, with their smoke points attached.
  - Clarified butter (ghee) (230°C/450°F)
  - Rice bran oil (250°C/490°F)
  - Refined safflower oil (265°C/510°F)
  - Soybean oil (230°C/450°F)
  - Refined avocado oil (270°C/520°F)

Preparation is king

- Preheat your air fryer! This is the simplest trick to giving you extra crispy foods, cooked through perfectly. If your air fryer doesn't have a preheat function, just turn it on to the right temperature while you prepare your ingredients. By the time you put your food in the air fryer, it will be at the right temperature, and it'll cook perfectly!

Know your air fryer

- It's important to know some simple things about your air fryer before you use it. For example – is it dishwasher safe?

Not all air fryer baskets are, and if you put it in the dishwasher to clean it, you could damage the non-stick material.

– Your air fryer may cook at a slightly different speed or may take longer than other air fryers to get to temperature. These are all things you'll come to know through using your air fryer more often but be aware that your cooking times may vary a little to ours.

Miscellaneous tips and tricks

– Don't overcrowd the basket

  • It can be tempting to pack food into your air fryer basket, particularly if you have a small one and you're cooking for a lot of people. Resist that urges! If you overcrowd the basket, your air fryer won't cook evenly, because the air won't be able to circulate properly. It's best to spread your food out and cook in batches.

– Shake the food

  • Removing the food from the air fryer halfway through cooking and shaking it around is a great way to redistribute the food and help to get the underside just as crispy as the topside!

- Add water to the bottom drawer

  - For anyone who's cooked high fat foods in their air fryer – like bacon for example – you'll be familiar with the white smoke that comes all too easily. A good way to mitigate this is to put a little water in the bottom tray beforehand.

- Get a quick read thermometer

  - If you're cooking meat, this is essential. Because your air fryer can cook the outside of your food very quickly, you may be fooled into thinking that a piece of meat is cooked the whole way through when it isn't. In order to make sure your food is cooked through, invest in a thermometer.

- Speed up the cleaning

  - If you want to speed up the cleaning process, line your basket with tinfoil or baking (parchment) paper. This will help make the cleaning process a whole lot easier.

So, with that section out of the way, even those of you that are completely new to the air frying game should be all caught up now. The truth is, using an air fryer is incredibly simple, and although there are a few unique issues that you might run into while using one, all of these problems have very simple solutions!

Without further ado, let's move on to the next (delicious) section of the book – the recipes.

Section Two: Recipes

Breakfast

Breakfast frittata

Serves: 2 People

Prep Time: 10 Minutes | Cook Time: 16 Minutes | Total Time: 26 Minutes

Calories: 315 | Net Carbs: 9g | Protein: 24g | Fat: 22g | Fiber: 2g

Ingredients

◆ 4 large eggs

◆ 4 tbsp milk of choice

◆ 35g // ½ cup cheddar cheese (grated)

◆ 50g // ¼ cup Feta cheese (crumbled)

◆ 15g // ½ cup spinach (roughly chopped)

◆ 1 large tomato (chopped)

◆ 1 tbsp fresh mixed herbs

◆ 2 spring (green) onions (finely chopped)

◆ Salt and pepper, to taste

◆ ½ tsp oil of choice

Also needed:
A springform cake tin that will fit into your air fryer basket

Instructions

1. Break the eggs into a small bowl and whisk together with the milk. Add the cheese, chopped tomato, spinach, onion, salt and pepper and spring onion. Mix together using a fork until all ingredients are fully combined.

2. Preheat your air fryer to 180°C (350°F). Line the cake tin with a sheet of baking paper and grease the sides of the tin using a little oil.

3. Pour the mixture into the cake tin and tilt the tin around so that the mixture is evenly distributed.

4. Cook for 12 minutes before checking to see if the frittata has cooked. If not, put back into the air fryer and continue checking at 1-minute intervals.

5. Leave to cool for 5 minutes, then run a knife around the sides of the cake tin, between the tin and the frittata. Loosen the frittata and tip onto a plate before slicing and serving.

Breakfast burrito

Serves: 6 People

Prep Time: 25 Minutes | Cook Time: 15 Minutes | Total Time: 40 Minutes

Calories: 492 | Net Carbs: 42g | Protein: 24g | Fat: 25g | Fiber: 2g

Ingredients

◆ 1 medium white potato

◆ 1 tbsp oil of choice

◆ 1 tsp salt

◆ 1 tsp pepper

◆ 225g // ½ lb.. sausage meat

◆ 6 flour tortillas (can be substituted for corn tortillas)

◆ 4 large eggs

◆ 60 ml // ¼ cup milk of choice

◆ 70g // 1 cup cheese (grated)

Instructions

1. Preheat your air fryer to 200 °C (400°F). Line the basket with a sheet of tin foil (aluminum foil). Warm a pan or skillet over a medium high heat.

2. Scrub the potatoes and chop them into cubes of about ¼ inch. Brush with oil, and then sprinkle with salt and pepper. Toss in the air fryer basket and cook for 8 minutes. Set to one side in a bowl. Turn down your air fryer to 380°F (190°C)

3. While the potatoes are cooking, put the sausage meat into the pan and cook until the meat has browned. Stir the sausage meat thoroughly while cooking, so that it crumbles. Pour into the same bowl as the potatoes, and then pour the cheese over the top.

4. In a jug, combine the eggs, salt, pepper and milk. Whisk well to make sure all ingredients are fully combined. Pour into the pan and cook in the leftover grease from the sausage meat. Stir quickly to scramble the eggs, before combining with the sausage meat and potatoes in the bowl. Mix all the ingredients together.

5. Divide the mixture between each of the tortillas before wrapping them tightly. Pin the edges of the tortilla down using toothpicks or broken bamboo skewers.

6. Brush or spray the burritos with oil and cook in the air fryer. Cook for 8 minutes, then remove from the air fryer and flip before cooking for a further 8 minutes.

7. Remove and serve immediately.

Hash browns

Serves: 4 people

Prep Time: 35 Minutes | Cook Time: 20 Minutes | Total Time: 55 Minutes

Calories: 280 | Net Carbs: 42g | Protein: 4g | Fat: 13g | Fiber: 4g

Ingredients

◈ 2 medium potatoes

◈ 2 tbsp oil of choice

◈ 1 tsp salt

◈ ½ tsp garlic powder

◈ ½ tsp onion powder

◈ ½ tsp black pepper

Instructions

1. Scrub the potatoes to clean them of any dirt. Use a grater to shred the potato, and then place in a bowl with cold water. Allow the potato shreds to soak for 30 minutes before draining.

2. Pre-heat your air fryer to 190°C (380°F). Line the basket of your air fryer with a layer of tinfoil (aluminum foil).

3. Dry the potato by pressing between layers of paper towel and squeezing the moisture from them. Try to dry them as much as you can.

4. Transfer the potatoes to a bowl and drizzle with oil. Add the seasoning and toss all the ingredients, making sure that all of the potato is covered.

5. Add the potato to the basket in a thin layer. Cook for 10 minutes, then remove the basket and toss the potato, breaking up any large pieces. Return to the air fryer and cook for another 10 minutes.

Marc Goodwin

Cinnamon rolls

Serves: 6 people

Prep Time: 20 Minutes | Cook Time: 15 Minutes | Total Time: 35 Minutes

Calories: 341 | Net Carbs: 44g | Protein: 3g | Fat: 17g | Fiber: 1g

Ingredients

To make the Cinnamon Filling

◆ 2 tbsp butter (melted)

◆ 1 tsp cinnamon (powdered)

◆ 110g // ½ cup brown sugar (can be substituted for caster sugar)

To make the Dough

◆ 1 125g plain // 1 cup (all purpose) flour

◆ 4 tsp granulated sugar (can be substituted for caster sugar)

◆ A pinch of salt

◆ 4 tbsp butter, (chilled and cubed)

◆ 1/8 tsp bicarbonate of soda (baking soda)

◆ 1 tsp baking powder

◆ 75ml // 1/3 cup milk (of your choice)

To make the Icing

◈ 1 tbsp butter (softened but not melted)

◈ 4 tbsp cream cheese

◈ ½ tsp vanilla extract (adjust according to taste)

◈ 65g // ½ cup icing sugar (confectioners' sugar)

Also needed: a round cake pan that will fit in the basket of your air fryer

Instructions

1. Grease the cake pan with a little butter or vegetable oil and set aside until needed later

2. In a microwave safe bowl, melt the butter in intervals of 30 seconds. Be careful not to overheat. Once melted, remove the bowl from the microwave and mix in the cinnamon and sugar. When mixed, set aside in the fridge while you make the dough.

3. Before making your dough, preheat your air fryer to 160°C (320°F) so that it's well heated by the time you need it.

4. In a large mixing bowl, combine the dried ingredients needed for the dough (as listed above. Mix them well with a whisk.

5. Cut the chilled butter into small cubes and add to the bowl. Using a fork, break the butter up and mash it into the dried ingredients until it resembles a crumbly mixture.

6. Stir in the milk slowly, adding a little bit at a time. By the time you have added all the milk, it should have turned into a lump of dough that you can roll.

7. Roll the dough out until it forms a ½ inch thick sheet. Spread the cinnamon filling mixture evenly across the dough sheet.

8. Carefully roll the sheet of dough into a log, similar to the way you would roll a roulade or sushi. Optionally, if you want the log to keep its shape a little better when you cut it, you can put it into the fridge for another 15 minutes to firm up.

9. Cut the dough into 6 even sections and place them into the cake pan, leaving as much space between them as possible. Place the cake tin in your air fryer and cook for between 10-14 minutes. We recommend checking them after 10 minutes, and then at 1-minute intervals after that.

10. While the cinnamon rolls are cooking, add the softened butter and cream cheese to a bowl and mix thoroughly. Then add the vanilla and icing sugar until mixed well into a glaze.

11. When the cinnamon rolls have finished cooking, take them out of the air fryer and allow to stand for 2 minutes before drizzling the icing over the top.

French toast

Serves: 4 People

Prep Time: 10 Minutes | Cook Time: 10 Minutes | Total Time: 20 Minutes

Calories: 180 | Net Carbs: 52g | Protein: 5g | Fat: 3g | Fiber: 2g

Ingredients

◈ 8 slices of thick toast

◈ 200 ml // 1 cup milk of choice

◈ 4 medium eggs

◈ 4 tbsp butter

◈ 50g // ¼ cup granulated sugar (can be substituted for caster sugar)

◈ 1 tbsp cinnamon

◈ 1 tsp vanilla extract

◈ Maple syrup (optional)

◈ Fresh berries (optional)

Instructions

1. Pre-heat your air fryer to 180°C (350°F). Line the basket of your air fryer with a sheet of baking paper.

2. Slice the bread into halves or thirds. Set to one side.

3. In a microwave safe bowl, melt the butter. Put the microwave on for 1 minute, and then continue to cook the butter in increments of 20 seconds until completely melted. Add the milk and vanilla and mix. Crack the eggs into the bowl and whisk until fully combined. Set to one side.

4. In a separate bowl, mix the sugar and cinnamon until combined.

5. Dip the bread into the egg mix until coated on both sides. Gently roll each piece of bread in the sugar mix.

6. Lay each piece of bread in the air fryer basket and cook for 6 minutes. After 6 minutes, remove and flip over onto the other side. Cook for a further 4 minutes and serve while hot with maple syrup and fresh berries

Marc Goodwin

Lunch

Empanadas

Serves: 8 People

Prep Time: 45 Minutes | Cook Time: 25 Minutes | Total Time: 65 Minutes

Calories: 215 | Net Carbs: 20g | Protein: 5g | Fat: 12g | Fiber: 1g

Ingredients

◈ 1 pack ready to roll puff pastry

◈ 1 tbsp oil of your choice

◈ 120g // ¼ lb. ground beef

◈ 40g // ¼ cup chopped brown onion (can be substituted for white onion)

◈ 40g // ¼ cup chopped bell pepper

◈ 1 tsp cumin

◈ ½ tsp smoked paprika

◈ ¼ tsp oregano

◈ ½ tsp salt

◈ ½ tsp black pepper

◈ 1 large egg

◈ 1 tbsp water

Instructions

1. Before cooking allow your pastry to sit for 15 minutes, giving it time to warm up a little. This gives the pasty time to soften up a little. If you try to roll out the pasty without letting it sit out on the side, it might crack.

2. Warm a pan over a high heat and add the oil to it. Add the meat and onion and cook until the beef begins to brown. Stir continuously while cooking.

3. Add the pepper and continue to stir. Cook for about 5 minutes before adding the seasonings.

4. Cook for a further five minutes before transferring the mixture into a bowl and setting it to one side to be used later.

5. Roll out the sheet of pasty. Use a pastry cutter or a ramekin to cut out rounds from the pasty sheet. These will be your empanada cases. Set each case to one side.

6. Preheat your air fryer to 200 °C (400°F). Lightly brush the air fryer basket with oil.

7. Divide the mixture up between your empanada cases. Place the mixture in the middle of each case.

8. Brush water around the top edge of each empanada case and then fold the case over on itself. Seal each empanada case by pressing the edges together using a fork.

9. In a jug, crack your egg and whisk until the yolk and egg whites have been broken up. Add 1 tbsp of water to the egg and mix again to create your egg wash. Brush the egg wash over the top of each empanada case.

10. Place the empanadas in your air fryer basket. Leave enough space between each empanada so the pastry can expand during the cooking process.

11. Cook the empanadas for 5 minutes before removing. Flip over and continue cooking for another 5 minutes. Serve while hot.

Sausage rolls

Serves: 4 People

Prep Time: 20 Minutes | Cook Time: 10 Minutes | Total Time: 30 Minutes

Calories: 525 | Net Carbs: 22g | Protein: 23g | Fat: 41g | Fiber: 3g

Ingredients

For the Pastry

❖ 225g // 1 cup plain (all purpose) flour

❖ 100g // ¼ cup butter (softened)

❖ 1 tbsp extra virgin olive oil

❖ 1 tbsp dried Italian herbs

❖ Pinch of salt

❖ Pinch of black pepper

❖ 1 cup water

For the Sausage

❖ 450g // 3 cups sausage meat

❖ 2 tsp oregano

❖ ½ tsp garlic powder

❖ ½ tsp onion powder

❖ Salt and pepper, to taste

❖ 1 medium egg

❖ ½ cup water

Instructions

1. Preheat your air fryer to 200°C (400°F). Line the basket of your air fryer with tin foil (aluminum foil).

2. Cut your butter into small cubes. Pour the butter and the flour into a large mixing bowl and rub the butter into the flour until it looks like breadcrumbs.

3. Add the oil, salt, pepper and mixed dry Italian herbs for flavor.

4. Add water a little bit at a time, kneading the flour until it begins to form a dough. Be careful when adding water as you don't want to make the dough too wet – you want to add just enough water to bind the dough together. If you accidentally add too much water, sprinkle a little more flour into the mix.

5. Once the dough is ready, roll it out until it is about ¼ inch thick.

6. In a bowl, mix the sausage meat and all other ingredients (except the egg and water). Mash the ingredients together using your hands and roll into a long sausage. Lay this along the middle of the pastry.

Marc Goodwin

7. Roll the pasty over itself and seal the edges together using a fork. In a small bowl, whisk the egg and water to create an egg wash. Brush over the top of the sausage roll. Slice the sausage roll into four separate rolls and place in the basket of the air fryer.

8. Air fry for 10 minutes. Serve hot.

Mini pizzas

Serves: 2 People

Prep Time: 10 Minutes | Cook Time: 5 Minutes | Total Time: 15 Minutes

Calories: 270 | Net Carbs: 35g | Protein: 13g | Fat: 11g | Fiber: 3g

Ingredients

◈ 2 English breakfast muffins (sliced)

◈ 1 tbsp tomato puree

◈ 115g // 1/2 cup mozzarella cheese (shredded)

◈ ¼ tsp dried mixed Italian herbs

◈ ¼ tsp garlic powder

◈ ¼ tsp onion powder

◈ 120g // ½ cup mini pepperoni pieces

Instructions

1. Pre-heat your air fryer to 200°C (390°F) and line the basket of your air fryer to catch any melted cheese that drips off the side of the pizzas. Slice the English breakfast muffins in half.

2. In a small bowl, mix the tomato puree with the dried herbs, onion powder and garlic powder. This makes your pizza sauce.

3. Use a knife to spread the pizza sauce across each side of the English muffins.

4. Sprinkle mozzarella cheese on top of the English muffins, and then add the pepperoni pieces.

5. Place the mini pizzas into your air fryer.

6. Air fry for 5 minutes. The cheese should melt and become bubbly, and the base should be crispy.

Fried chicken sandwich

Serves: 4 people

Prep Time: 40 Minutes | Cook Time: 20 Minutes | Total Time: 60 Minutes

Calories: 495 | Net Carbs: 52g | Protein: 31g | Fat: 14g | Fiber: 6.2g

Ingredients

- 120 ml // ½ cup pickle juice (can be substituted for white vinegar and salt)
- 2 chicken breasts (halved)
- 2 large eggs
- 120ml // ½ cup milk
- 1 tsp paprika
- 1 tsp salt
- ½ tsp garlic powder (adjust according to taste)
- ½ tsp black pepper
- 125g // 1 cup plain (all purpose) flour
- 1 tbsp icing sugar (confectioners' sugar)
- 4 burger buns (lightly toasted)
- 8 pickle slices (optional)
- 2 beef tomatoes (sliced, optional)
- 4 romaine lettuce leaves (shredded, optional)

Instructions

1. In a large bowl, combine the chicken breasts with the pickle juice (or salt and vinegar if no pickle juice is available). Cover with cling film and set aside in the fridge for a minimum of 20 minutes

2. In another bowl, combine the eggs and milk. Whisk until they are fully mixed together, but be careful not to overmix them (we prefer a hand whisk or fork for this, rather than an electric whisk)

3. In a mixing bowl, add the dried ingredients – paprika, salt, pepper, garlic powder, sugar and flour. Mix them well.

4. Remove the chicken from the fridge, and discard of the brine safely. Using tongs, dip the chicken in the egg and milk mixture.

5. Roll the chicken breasts into the flour and spice mixture, making sure that each chicken breast is well covered.

6. Place the chicken breasts into your air fryer basket, taking care to leave space between them. Add a little cooking oil over the top, preferably using a mister.

7. Cook the chicken for six minutes and then remove from the

air fryer. Flip each chicken breast, spray with a little more cooking oil, and then place the chicken back into the air fryer for another 6 minutes.

8. To crisp up the outside of the chicken before serving, turn up the temperature to 200°C (400°F). Cook for 4 minutes on each side and add a little extra time if the chicken is still pink on the inside. During this step, lightly toast your burger buns.

9. Serve the chicken in the buns, with additional toppings if desired.

Crab cakes

Serves: 4 People

Prep Time: 60 Minutes | Cook Time: 15 Minutes | Total Time: 75 Minutes

Calories: 210 | Net Carbs: 18g | Protein: 32g | Fat: 12g | Fiber: 1g

Ingredients

◈ 340g // 12oz. canned white crab meat

◈ 50g // ½ cup panko breadcrumbs (can be substituted for any other dried breadcrumbs)

◈ ¼ cup celery (finely chopped)

◈ 1 tbsp spring onion (green onion)

◈ 1 tbsp mayonnaise

◈ 1 tbsp oil of choice

◈ 1 large egg

◈ ½ tsp celery salt

◈ ½ tsp ground bay leaves

◈ 1 tsp smoked paprika

◈ ½ tsp black pepper

◈ Pinch of cayenne pepper

◈ Pinch of cinnamon

◈ Pinch of powdered nutmeg

◈ Pinch of powdered ginger

◈ Pinch of salt

◈ Pinch of black pepper

◈ Lemon (optional)

Instructions

1. In a large bowl, crack the egg and whisk until broken up. Add the seasoning, oil and mayonnaise and mix until fully combined.

2. Add the spring onion and celery to the bowl, followed by the crab meat. Mix into the egg and mayonnaise mixture until fully incorporated.

3. Lastly, add the breadcrumbs and fold into the mixture. Cover the mixing bowl and put aside in the fridge for an hour.

4. Before removing from the fridge, preheat your air fryer to 200°C (400°F). Line the basket of your air fryer with a sheet of baking (parchment) paper.

5. Divide the crab meat out into patties (the mixture should make 12 patties – 3 for each person).

6. Lay the crab cakes into the basket, leaving space between each one. Cook for 7 minutes and then remove. Flip the cakes over and cook for a further 8 minutes until golden and crispy. Serve with lemon juice.

Marc Goodwin

Dinner

Corn dogs

Serves: 8 People

Prep Time: 15 Minutes | Cook Time: 10 Minutes | Total Time: 25 Minutes

Calories: 135 | Net Carbs: 18g | Protein: 7g | Fat: 3g | Fiber: 2g

Ingredients

◈ 4 hot dogs

◈ 100g // ¾ cup cornmeal

◈ 100g plain // ¾ cup (all purpose) flour*

◈ 1 ½ tsp baking powder

◈ ½ tsp bicarbonate of soda (baking soda)

◈ 1 tsp granulated sugar (can be substituted for caster sugar)

◈ ½ tsp salt

◈ 175 ml // buttermilk

◈ 2 large eggs

◈ 200g // 1 ½ cups panko breadcrumbs (can be substituted for other dried breadcrumbs)

Also required: bamboo skewers, tall glass (like a highball or half pint glass)

---

* Keep aside extra flour to use for rolling

Instructions

1. Combine the flour, baking powder, bicarbonate of soda, sugar, salt and cornmeal in a large mixing bowl. Make sure they are well combined.

2. In a separate, smaller bowl, crack the eggs. Whisk using a fork until the eggs are broken up, and then add the buttermilk. Whisk to combine fully.

3. Use a spoon to create a well in the middle of the dried ingredients, and carefully pour the wet ingredients into this. Use a spoon to mix all the ingredients. Scrape down the sides of the bowl to make sure no flour sticks to the edge.

4. Pour this batter into a tall glass, filling it about ¾ full. Be careful not to overfill the glass, as you might end up spilling mixture out when you dip the hot dog in.

5. Pour the breadcrumbs into a shallow bowl or plate. Put to one side. Sprinkle some flour on a separate plate and set to one side as well.

6. Pre-heat your air fryer to 375°F (190°C). Line the basket of your air fryer with baking (parchment) paper.

7. Cut the hot dogs in half, and poke bamboo skewers through them until they are about ¾ of the way through the hot dogs.

8. Roll the hot dogs in the flour so they are lightly covered. Once covered in flour dip them in the batter, and then roll in the breadcrumbs. Use your hands to press the breadcrumbs into the batter if needed.

9. Spray or brush cooking oil on the corn dogs and put them in the air fryer basket. Leave space between each corn dog.

10. Cook the corn dogs for 5 minutes. Remove from the air fryer, flip to the other side and then cook for a further 5 minutes. Serve hot.

Marc Goodwin

Spicy Tofu

Serves: 5 People

Prep Time: 15 Minutes | Cook Time: 15 Minutes | Total Time: 30 Minutes

Calories: 170 | Net Carbs: 22g | Protein: 8g | Fat: 8g | Fiber: 2g

Ingredients

◈ 1 pack of super firm tofu (about 280g // 10 oz.)

◈ 35g // ¼ cup cornstarch (can be substituted for tapioca powder or arrowroot powder)

◈ 1 tbsp oil of choice

◈ 55ml // ¼ cup dark soy sauce

◈ 2 tbsp sweet chili sauce

◈ 1 tbsp white rice wine vinegar

◈ 1 ½ tbsp brown sugar

◈ 2 garlic cloves (minced) (can be substituted for 2 tsp of pre-minced garlic)

◈ 1 tsp fresh ginger (grated)

- ◈ Pinch of red pepper flakes, such as cayenne or gochugaru (optional)
- ◈ 1 tsp sesame oil
- ◈ ½ tsp sesame seeds
- ◈ 2 spring onions (green onions) (finely sliced)

Instructions

1. Drain the block of tofu out of the packaging and wrap in several layers of paper towels. Lay a chopping board on top of the tofu, and then place a heavy pot on top. This presses the water out of the tofu, which helps it to take in more of the flavor later on in the recipe. Leave the tofu wrapped like this for at least 30 minutes (preferably an hour).

2. Cut the tofu into ½ inch cubes.

3. Decant the cornstarch (or substitute) into a zip loc bag and add the tofu. Close the bag and shake, making sure that all of the tofu is covered by the cornstarch. If there is an excess amount of cornstarch on the tofu, shake a little off before drizzling oil over the top.

4. Warm a pan over a medium high heat. Preheat your air fryer to 190°C (370°F) ().

5. Line the basket with a sheet of baking (parchment) paper. Add the tofu into the basket in a single layer, taking care to not overcrowd the basket. Cook in batches if needed.

6. Cook the tofu for 7 minutes. Remove the basket, shake the tofu and spray a little oil onto the tofu before cooking for a further 8 minutes.

7. While the tofu cooks in the air fryer, add the soy sauce, ginger, sweet chili sauce, vinegar, brown sugar and red pepper flakes (if using) to the pan. Bring these ingredients to the boil, and then reduce to a simmer. Add the tofu and stir thoroughly.

8. Slice the spring onions finely and sprinkle on top, along with sesame seeds and sesame oil.

Marc Goodwin

Honey glazed fried salmon

Serves: 4 People

Prep Time: 5 Minutes | Cook Time: 8 Minutes | Total Time: 13 Minutes

Calories: 282 | Net Carbs: 4g | Protein: 32g | Fat: 10g | Fiber: 1g

Ingredients

◈ 4 salmon fillets with the skin on

◈ 2 tbsp soy sauce

◈ 1 tbsp honey

◈ Salt to taste

◈ Cracked black pepper

◈ 1 tsp sesame seeds

Instructions

1. Preheat your air fryer to 190°C (375°F).

2. Lightly brush each salmon fillet with soy sauce and sprinkle a little salt and pepper over the salmon fillets.

3. Cook in the air fryer for 6 minutes. Remove from the air fryer and brush with honey to glaze. Sprinkle the sesame seeds, along with a little more salt and pepper. Place back in the air fryer and cook for a further 2 minutes. Use a thermometer to check if the fish is cooked to 63°C (145°F). Serve with salad and potatoes.

Taquitos

Serves: 10 People (1 Taquito each)

Prep Time: 30 Minutes | Cook Time: 30 Minutes | Total Time: 60 Minutes

Calories: 168 | Net Carbs: 21g | Protein: 16g | Fat: 8g | Fiber: 3g

Ingredients

◈ 2 large eggs

◈ 50g // ½ cup breadcrumbs

◈ 3 tbsp taco seasoning

◈ 450g // 1 lb. ground beef

◈ 10 corn tortillas (can be substituted with flour tortillas)

◈ Salsa Verde (for topping)

◈ Guacamole (for topping)

Instructions

1. Preheat your air fryer to 180°C (350°F).

2. In a large mixing bowl, break the egg and whisk using a fork until the yolk and egg white have been combined.

3. Add the breadcrumbs and the taco seasoning and whisk thoroughly. Lastly, add the beef and combine fully with the seasoning.

4. Place the tortillas on a microwave safe plate. Warm the tortillas for 30 seconds in the microwave.

5. Divide the beef mixture between the six tortillas. Roll each tortilla up tightly, and pin using a toothpick to secure the rolls.

6. Brush lightly with oil before laying in the air fryer basket. Cook for 6 minutes before removing from the air fryer. Flip over and cook for another 6 minutes, so the taquitos are crispy on both sides. Serve while hot with salsa Verde and guacamole.

Keto friendly meatballs

Serves: 4 People

Prep Time: 30 Minutes | Cook Time: 8 Minutes | Total Time: 38 Minutes

preCalories: 410 | Net Carbs: 8g | Protein: 34g | Fat: 27g | Fiber: 3g

Ingredients

For the Meatballs

- ❖ 65g // ½ cup parmesan cheese (grated)
- ❖ 65g // ½ cup mozzarella cheese (shredded)
- ❖ 1 large egg
- ❖ 2 tbsp double cream
- ❖ 1 garlic clove (minced) (can be substituted for a tsp preminced garlic)
- ❖ 450g // 1 lb. ground beef

For the Sauce

- ❖ 240ml // 8oz. passata sauce
- ❖ 1 tsp garlic powder
- ❖ 1 tsp mixed Italian herbs
- ❖ 2 tbsp red pesto
- ❖ 4 tbsp double cream

Instructions

1. Preheat your air fryer to 180°C (350°F). Line the bottom of the basket with a sheet of baking (parchment) paper. Warm a saucepan over a medium high heat.

2. Crack an egg into a large bowl and whisk until the yolk and white are broken up. Add the cheese, garlic and cream and mix well until fully combined.

3. Add the ground beef and mix using your hands. Divide into golf ball sized pieces and roll into balls.

4. Place in the air fryer in a single layer. Cook for 4 minutes, then remove the basket from the air fryer and cook for a further 4 minutes.

5. While the meatballs cook, mix the passata and cream in the saucepan and bring to a simmer stir in the pesto, garlic powder and Italian herbs. Pour over the meatballs before serving.

Marc Goodwin

Stuffed chicken breasts

Serves: 4 People

Prep Time: 10 Minutes | Cook Time: 15 Minutes | Total Time: 25 Minutes

Calories: 409 | Net Carbs: 6g | Protein: 43g | Fat: 22g | Fiber: 2g

Ingredients

◈ 4 boneless chicken breasts

◈ 1 tbsp extra virgin olive oil

◈ 1 tsp smoked paprika

◈ 1 tsp salt

◈ ½ tsp garlic powder

◈ ½ tsp onion powder

◈ 115g // 4 oz. cream cheese (softened)

◈ 35 g // ¼ cup parmesan cheese (grated)

◈ 2 tbsp mayonnaise

◈ 45g // 1 ½ cups fresh spinach (roughly chopped)

◈ 2 fresh cloves of garlic (minced) (can be substituted for 2 tsp preminced garlic)

◈ Pinch of red pepper flakes (optional, to taste)

Instructions

1. Preheat your air fryer to 190°C (375°F). Line the basket of your air fryer with a sheet of baking (parchment) paper.

2. Use a sharp knife to cut into the side of each chicken breast. Cut about ¾ of the way through the chicken breast, creating the pocket that will later be stuffed.

3. Brush or drizzle olive oil on either side of the chicken breasts

4. In a small bowl, combine the paprika, garlic powder, onion powder and ½ tsp of the salt. Sprinkle or rub this over each side of the chicken breasts.

5. In another bowl, combine the cream cheese, parmesan cheese, spinach, minced garlic and mayonnaise (and red pepper flakes, if using). Add the other ½ tsp of salt. Mix and combine fully using a spoon.

6. Divide the mixture between each of the 4 chicken breasts and use a spoon to fill the pockets created earlier.

7. Lay the chicken breasts in the air fryer basket, taking care not to overcrowd it. Cook for 15 minutes and check that the internal temperature of the chicken is at least 165°F (75°C). If not, cook for a further 5 minutes and check again.

8. Serve immediately.

Jamaican Style Pork Chops

Serves: 4 People

Prep Time: 35 Minutes | Cook Time: 10 Minutes | Total Time: 31 Minutes

Calories: 372 | Net Carbs: 24g | Protein: 22g | Fat: 12g | Fiber: 4g

Ingredients

◈ 1 tbsp butter

◈ ¼ cup canned peaches

◈ 4 boneless pork chops

◈ 4 tsp jerk seasoning

◈ 1 tsp salt

◈ 1 tsp black pepper

◈ 1 red bell pepper

◈ 1 yellow bell pepper

Instructions

1. Sprinkle the jerk seasoning, salt and pepper on either side of the pork chops. Cover and put in the fridge for 30 minutes to allow the flavors to marinade a little. If possible, leave for a little longer.

2. When ready to cook, pre-heat your air fryer to 180°C (350°F).

3. Soften the butter in the microwave for about 30 seconds and then stir in the peaches. Set to one side.

4. Place the pork chops in the air fryer for 2 minutes before removing and flipping to the other side. Cook for another 2 minutes and then remove and set aside.

5. Slice the peppers into long, thin strips. Place on a sheet of baking paper and then put into the air fryer basket. Cook for 3 minutes, then remove and shake the basket to redistribute the food. Cook for another 3 minutes.

6. Add the pork chops back to the air fryer and put the butter mixture over the top of each pork chop. Cook for another 2 minutes and serve immediately.

Stuffed red pepper

Serves: 4 People

Prep Time: 15 Minutes | Cook Time: 16 Minutes | Total Time: 31 Minutes

Calories: 163 | Net Carbs: 24g | Protein: 5g | Fat: 5g | Fiber: 4g

Ingredients

◈ 4 red bell peppers

◈ 425g // 15 oz. tinned chopped tomatoes

◈ 200g // 1 cup cooked long grain rice

◈ 1 can kidney beans

◈ 1 tbsp dried mixed Italian herbs

◈ 114g // ½ cup mozzarella cheese (shredded)

◈ 1 tbsp parmesan cheese (grated)

Instructions

1. Pre-heat your air fryer to 180°C (360°F). Line the basket of your air fryer with a sheet of tin foil (aluminum foil).

2. Slice of the top of each bell pepper. Remove the cores of each pepper and scoop out any seeds. Finely chop up the tops of each of the bell peppers and put into a bowl.

3. Mix the sliced-up pepper, tinned tomatoes, rice, beans and herbs together.

4. Divide the mixture between each of the bell peppers. Place in the air fryer basket and cook for 12 minutes.

5. Remove from the air fryer and sprinkle cheese over the top of each bell pepper. Cook for a further 4 minutes and serve immediately.

Snacks and sides

Egg rolls

Serves: 3 People

Prep Time: 10 Minutes | Cook Time: 9 Minutes | Total Time: 19 Minutes

Calories: 82 | Net Carbs: 6g | Protein: 1g | Fat: 5g | Fiber: 2g

Ingredients

◈ 6 egg roll wrappers

◈ 175g // 3 cups cabbage (shredded)

◈ 25g // ¼ cup carrot (shredded)

◈ 1 tbsp sesame oil

◈ 2 tsp fresh grated ginger

◈ 1 glove garlic (minced – can be substituted for 1 tsp preminced garlic)

◈ 1 tsp soy sauce

◈ ½ tsp black pepper

◈ 2 spring (green) onions (finely chopped)

◈ 1 tsp oil of choice

Instructions

1. Preheat your air fryer to 180°C (360°F). preheat a pan over a medium high heat.

2. Add the sesame oil, ginger, garlic, cabbage and carrot to the pan and cook until the cabbage softens and wilts. Then add the onion, soy sauce and pepper. Cook for an additional 2 minutes and then transfer to a bowl.

3. Assemble your egg rolls: place an egg roll wrapper at an angle, with the bottom corner facing towards you. Place the filling in the bottom third of the wrapper. Roll the bottom corner of the egg roll up towards the middle of the wrapper. Then fold the sides of the egg roll in towards the center. Finally brush a little water along the top edge of the wrapper and fold over the egg roll, patting down to secure it.

4. Brush oil over each egg roll, and along the basket of your air fryer. Place the egg rolls in a single layer and cook for 6 minutes. Remove from the air fryer and cook for a further 3 minutes before serving hot.

Mac and cheese bites

Serves: 4 People

Prep Time: 20 Minutes | Cook Time: 20 Minutes | Total Time: 40 Minutes

Calories: 552 | Net Carbs: 76g | Protein: 22g | Fat: 21g | Fiber: 4g

Ingredients

◈ 800g // 4 cups leftover macaroni and cheese (or instant macaroni and cheese, premade)

◈ 130g // 1 cup panko breadcrumbs (can be substituted for any other dried breadcrumb)

◈ 3 tbsp plain (all purpose) flour

◈ 1 tsp salt

◈ 1 tsp black pepper

◈ 1 tsp smoked paprika

◈ 1 tsp garlic powder

◈ 1 tsp onion powder

◈ 2 large eggs

◈ 1 tbsp milk

Instructions

1. Preheat your oven to 200°C (400°F). Preheat your air fryer to 370°F (180°C). Line the bottom of your air fryer basket with a sheet of baking paper.

2. Spread the breadcrumbs out across the baking sheet in a thin layer. Bake in the oven for 2 minutes, then remove from the oven. Shake the breadcrumbs to redistribute them and add back to the oven for a further 3 minutes. They should come out a golden brown when toasted. Transfer into a bowl and mix with half of the pepper, salt, paprika, garlic and onion powder.

3. Use a tablespoon to divide the macaroni and cheese mixture. Roll into balls that are about the same size as golf balls.

4. Pour the flour into a small bowl. Add the other half of the seasonings to the flour and mix carefully. In a second bowl, combine the eggs and milk. Whisk well using a fork to break up the eggs and mix them fully with the milk.

5. One by one, roll the macaroni bites in the flour. Make sure they are fully coated, and then dip in the egg mixture. Finally, roll in the breadcrumbs before transferring into the air fryer basket.

6. Brush or spray with oil and cook for 6 minutes. Remove the air fryer basket, flip over each of the macaroni bites and cook for a further 4 minutes. Serve immediately.

Marc Goodwin

Roasted chickpeas

Serves: 4 people

Prep Time: 10 Minutes | Cook Time: 15 Minutes | Total Time: 25 minutes

Calories: 264 | Net Carbs: 34g | Protein: 10g | Fat: 5g | Fiber: 7g

Ingredients

◈ 540g // 19oz. canned chickpeas

◈ 1 tbsp oil of choice

◈ 1 tsp salt

◈ ½ tsp garlic powder

◈ ½ tsp onion powder

◈ ½ tsp paprika

◈ Pinch of cayenne pepper

Instructions

1. Preheat your air fryer to 200°C (400°F).

2. Drain the chickpeas and rinse in cold water. Pat dry using paper towel and transfer into a mixing bowl.

3. Add the spices and oil to the bowl and toss well. Add to the air fryer and cook for 15 minutes. At 5-minute intervals remove the basket and shake well.

4. Sprinkle with a little more salt and pepper before serving.

Buffalo cauliflower bites

Serves: 4 People

Prep Time: 45 Minutes | Cook Time: 15 Minutes | Total Time: 60 minutes

Calories: 210 | Net Carbs: 6g | Protein: 6g | Fat: 16g | Fiber: 3g

Ingredients

◈ 800g //5 cups cauliflower (cut into florets)

◈ 2 tbsp butter (melted)

◈ 1 tbsp oil of choice

◈ 150g // ½ cup hot sauce of your choice

◈ 70g // ½ cup plain (all purpose) flour

◈ 3 tbsp dried parsley

◈ ½ tbsp garlic powder

◈ ½ tbsp onion powder

◈ 1 tsp salt

Instructions

1. Chop the cauliflower head into florets and set to one side in a mixing bowl.

2. In a smaller microwave safe bowl, melt the butter in the microwave. This should take about 1 minute.

3. Add the oil and hot sauce to the butter. Mix until fully combined. Pour this over the cauliflower and mix well so the cauliflower is fully coated. Cover the cauliflower and leave to sit in the fridge for 30 minutes.

4. Before removing the cauliflower from the fridge, preheat your air fryer to 180°C (350°F). Line the basket of your air fryer with a sheet of baking (parchment) paper.

5. Combine the seasoning and flour in a small mixing bowl. Sprinkle this over the cauliflower, mixing gently as you do. Make sure the cauliflower is completely covered.

6. Add to the air fryer basket. Be careful to not overcrowd the basket, as the cauliflower won't crisp up if you do.

7. Cook for 15 minutes. At 5-minute intervals, remove the basket from your air fryer and shake to redistribute your food. Serve while hot.

Spicy sweet potato fries

Serves: 3 People

Prep Time: 10 Minutes | Cook Time: 25 Minutes | Total Time: 35 Minutes

Calories: 135 | Net Carbs: 26g | Protein: 5g | Fat: 6g | Fiber: 1g

Ingredients

◈ 3 sweet potatoes

◈ ½ tbsp oil of choice

◈ ½ tbsp chili oil

◈ 1 tsp garlic powder

◈ 1 tsp onion powder

◈ ½ tsp ground coriander

◈ ½ tsp salt

◈ ½ tsp smoked paprika

Instructions

1. Pre-heat your air fryer to 200°C (400°F). Line the basket of the air fryer with a sheet of tin foil.

2. Wash and scrub the sweet potatoes. Slice into 1/3-inch strips and toss with the oils. Cook in the air fryer for 18 minutes. The fries should be starting to brown.

3. Remove the fries and add back to the bowl. This time, toss with the spices, before adding them back to the air fryer. Cook for another 6 minutes. Serve immediately, with salsa, guacamole or sour cream.

Potato chips

Serves: 8 People

Prep Time: 25 Minutes | Cook Time: 15 Minutes | Total Time: 40 Minutes

Calories: 172 | Net Carbs: 20g | Protein: 1g | Fat: 8g | Fiber: 1g

Ingredients

◈ 4 white potatoes

◈ ¼ cup oil of choice

◈ 1 tsp sea salt

◈ 1 tsp cracked black pepper

Instructions

1. Fill a bowl with cold water and set to one side. Scrub the potatoes and slice as thinly as possible. Add the slices to the bowl and allow them to soak for 20 minutes.

2. Preheat the air fryer to 180°C (375°F). Line the basket with baking paper.

3. Remove the slices from the bowl of water and pat them dry using paper towel. Add the oil, salt and pepper to a clean bowl and then toss the potato slices in the mixture. Make sure they are fully coated.

4. Add the slices to the air fryer basket. If you need to weigh them down, stick toothpicks through the slices and into the baking paper.

5. Serve while hot.

Desserts

Blueberry mini muffins

Serves: 3 People

Prep Time: 20 minutes | Cook Time: 17 Minutes | Total Time: 37 Minutes

Calories: 45 | Net Carbs: 7g | Protein: 0.5g | Fat: 2g | Fiber: 0g

Ingredients

- ◈ 80g // 2/3 cup plain (all purpose) flour
- ◈ ½ tsp baking powder
- ◈ 65g // 1/3 cup granulated sugar (can be substituted for caster sugar)
- ◈ 80ml // 1/3 cup oil of your choice
- ◈ 1 medium egg
- ◈ 2 tbsp water
- ◈ ½ tsp vanilla extract
- ◈ ½ tsp fresh lemon juice
- ◈ 75g // ½ cup frozen blueberries
- ◈ Pinch of salt

Also needed: reusable silicone muffin cases

Instructions

1. Preheat your air fryer to 175°C (350°F).

2. Mix the flour, baking powder and sugar together in a mixing bowl. In a separate bowl, mix the egg, lemon juice, vanilla extract, oil and water together.

3. Using a spoon, create a well in the middle of the dried ingredients. Carefully pour the wet ingredients into the dried ingredients and mix. Before dividing the mixture into the muffin cases, mix the blueberries into the batter.

4. Carefully split the batter across each of the muffin cases. Leave a little space at the top for when the muffins expand.

5. Place in the air fryer and cook for 15 Minutes. Check to see if they are cooked by putting a toothpick into the middle of one of the muffins. If it comes out clean, remove the muffins and allow to cool on a rack.

Churros and chocolate

Serves: 8 People

Prep Time: 15 Minutes | Cook Time: 10 Minutes | Total Time: 25 Minutes

Calories: 215 | Net Carbs: 32g | Protein: 3g | Fat: 11g | Fiber: 1g

Ingredients

For the Churros

◈ 240ml // 1 cup water

◈ 75g // 1/3 cup butter (cubed)

◈ 25g // 2 tbsp granulated sugar (can be substituted for caster sugar)

◈ ½ tsp salt

◈ 130g // 1 cup plain (all purpose) flour

◈ 2 large eggs

◈ 1 tsp vanilla extract

◈ Oil of choice

For the Cinnamon Coating

◈ 100g // ½ cup granulated sugar (can be substituted for caster sugar)

◈ ¾ tsp cinnamon powder

Instructions

1. Line a baking tray with a sheet of baking paper and warm a saucepan over a medium high heat.

2. Add the water, butter, sugar and salt to the pan and bring to a simmer. Stir constantly using a spoon or spatula to stop a film from forming over the top. Slowly add the flour, bit by bit to the mixture and continue to stir. As you continue to do this a dough should form.

3. Allow to cool for 5 minutes in a mixing bowl.

4. Crack the eggs into a jug and mix with a fork until the eggs are completely broken up. Pour into the mixing bowl and use an electric whisk to combine with the rest of the ingredients.

5. Transfer this mixture into a piping bag – make sure the piping bag is using a fixture with ridges on it, as this is important for the topping.

6. Carefully pipe the churros out onto the baking paper. Because of the thickness of the batter, you will have to cut the end of each churro from the piping bag using a pair of kitchen scissors or a knife.

7. Refrigerate the churros for 1 hour.

8. When ready to cook, preheat your air fryer to 190°C (375°F). Line the basket of your air fryer with another sheet of baking paper.

9. Brush each of the churros with a little oil and transfer to the air fryer basket. Fry for 10 minutes until golden and crispy.

10. While the churros are cooking, add the cinnamon and sugar to a bowl. Mix well using a fork.

11. As soon as they come out of the air fryer, dip the churros in the sugar mixture and roll them around to fully coat. Serve warm.

Fudgy chocolate brownies

Serves: 9 People

Prep Time: 10 Minutes | Cook Time: 15 Minutes | Total Time: 25 Minutes

Calories: 265 | Net Carbs: 32g | Protein: 5g | Fat: 17g | Fiber: 2g

Ingredients

◈ 8 tbsp butter (melted)

◈ 30g // 1 oz. unsweetened cooking chocolate

◈ 85g // 2/3 cup unsweetened cocoa powder

◈ 45g // 1/3 cup plain (all purpose) flour

◈ 200g // 1 cup caster sugar (can be substituted for granulated sugar)

◈ ½ tsp salt

◈ 2 large eggs

◈ 1 tsp vanilla extract

Also needed: cake tin (preferably springform)

Instructions

1. Preheat your air fryer to 150°C (310°F). Line the base of your cake tin with a sheet of baking (parchment) paper. Grease the sides of the tin with a little oil or butter.

2. Break the chocolate into small pieces and add to a microwave safe bowl with the butter. Microwave until you see the butter and chocolate begin to melt, then remove from microwave and stir. Repeat this process, checking on the butter and chocolate in 30 second increments until fully melted.

3. Crack the eggs into the bowl and mix well stir the rest of the ingredients in to create a batter. Mix until smooth and scrape down the sides of the bowls to make sure there's no flour or cocoa powder on the sides of the bowl.

4. Pour the batter into the cake tin. Cook for 18 minutes and remove. Check that the brownies are cooked by sticking a toothpick or knife into the middle of the brownies. If it comes out clean remove and leave to cool. If batter comes off on the knife or toothpick, put back into the oven for another 2 minutes, then check again.

5. Leave to cool for 20 minutes. Run the knife around the edge of the cake tin and then rest the brownies on a wire rack. Serve with vanilla ice cream.

Cookies

Serves: 16 People (1 cookie each)

Prep Time: 80 Minutes | Cook Time: 5 Minutes | Total Time: 85 Minutes

Calories: 220 | Net Carbs: 25g | Protein: 2g | Fat: 13g | Fiber: 1g

Ingredients

- ◈ 110g // ½ cup butter
- ◈ 50g // ¼ cup granulated sugar (can be substituted for caster sugar)
- ◈ 110g // ½ cup brown sugar
- ◈ 1 large egg
- ◈ 1 tsp vanilla extract
- ◈ 1 tsp bicarbonate of soda (baking soda)
- ◈ 1 tsp sea salt
- ◈ 200g // 1 ½ cups plain (all purpose) flour
- ◈ 2 cups dark chocolate chips

Instructions

1. Add the butter to a microwave safe bowl and microwave for 15 seconds, so it is just starting to melt.

2. Add the brown and white sugar to the bowl and cream together.

3. Crack an egg into a jug, and whisk with a fork until well broken up. Add the vanilla extract and stir well.

4. Combine with the butter and sugar and mix thoroughly before adding the flour and bicarbonate of soda. Lastly, add the chocolate chips and stir in until all ingredients are fully combined.

5. Cover the mixing bowl and leave in the fridge for 1 hour.

6. When you take the cookie dough out of the freezer, preheat your air fryer to (150°C (300°F). Line the bottom of your basket with baking (parchment) paper.

7. Spoon out the dough, dividing it into portions that are about the size of a golf ball. Add them into the basket, leaving plenty of space between each cookie as they will spread out during the baking process.

8. Bake for 8 minutes before removing. Allow the cookies to rest for 5 minutes, then carefully remove and allow to finish cooling on a wire rack while you cook the rest of the cookies. Repeat in batches until all cookies have been baked.

Marc Goodwin

Lemon cake

Serves: 8 People

Prep Time: 10 Minutes | Cook Time: 20 Minutes | Total Time: 30 Minutes

Calories: 184 | Net Carbs: 24g | Protein: 2g | Fat: 6g | Fiber: 1g

Ingredients

◈ 2 large eggs

◈ 150g // 2/3 cup butter

◈ 120g // ¼ cup flour

◈ 75g // 1/3 cup granulated sugar (can be substituted for caster sugar)

◈ 2 tbsp fresh lemon juice

◈ 1 ½ tsp baking powder

◈ 1 tsp vanilla extract

◈ Pinch of salt

Also needed: Cake tin (preferably spring form)

Instructions

1. Preheat your air fryer to 160°C (320°F). Line the base of your cake tin with a sheet of baking paper and grease the sides with butter or oil.

2. Soften the butter in the microwave, cooking in 10 second increments. Combine with the sugar and vanilla extract using an electric whisk, until it creates a creamy mixture. Do not over mix.

3. Crack the eggs into a jug and whisk using a fork. Once fully broken up add the lemon juice and pour into the mixing bowl and whisk together.

4. Add the flour, baking powder and salt to the mixing bowl. Mix well and scrape down the sides to make sure no flour is left behind.

5. Pour into the cake tin and smooth down using a spatula, knife or spoon. Cook in the air fryer for 20 minutes. Check to see whether the cake has cooked by inserting a bamboo skewer or knife into the middle of the cake. If the skewer comes out clean, tip the cake onto a wire rack and leave to cool for 20 minutes.

Marc Goodwin

Apple Fritters

Serves: 12 people

Prep Time: 20 Minutes | Cook Time: 6 Minutes | Total Time: 26 Minutes

Calories: 100 | Net Carbs: 17g | Protein: 2g | Fat: 3g | Fiber: 1g

Ingredients

For the Apple Fritters

◈ 2 large apples (cored)

◈ 25g // 1/8 cup caster sugar (can be substituted for granulated sugar)

◈ 1 tsp baking powder

◈ ½ tsp salt

◈ ½ tsp cinnamon powder

◈ ¼ tsp nutmeg powder

◈ 125g // 1 cup plain flour

◈ 75ml // 1/3 cup milk

◈ 2 tbsp butter (melted)

◈ ½ tsp lemon juice

◈ 1 large egg

For the Cinnamon Icing

◈ 65g // ½ cup icing sugar (confectioners' sugar)

◈ 2 tbsp milk (any kind)

◈ Pinch of salt

◈ ½ tsp cinnamon powder

Marc Goodwin

Instructions

1. Remove the cores of the apples and cut them into small cubes. Refrigerate them in a covered bowl until needed.

2. In a large mixing bowl, combine the dried ingredients and mix well.

3. Microwave the butter in increments of 30 seconds to melt it. Once melted, add the milk, egg and lemon juice to the butter and mix with a fork or whisk. Then tip the wet ingredients into the large mixing bowl with the dried ingredients. Gently whisk the ingredients together into a thick batter but be careful not to overmix.

4. Tip the apples into the mixing bowl and then fold the pieces into the batter. Put the apple fritter mixture in the fridge for a minimum of 10 minutes.

5. When ready to eat the fritters, preheat your air fryer to 190°C (370°F), and place a sheet of baking paper on the bottom of the basket.

6. Using a tablespoon, scoop out the apple fritters into the basket. Each apple fritter should be about 2 tablespoons worth of batter. Cook for 6 minutes.

7. While the apple fritters are cooking, use the time to make the glaze. In a small bowl, mix the sugar, cinnamon, milk and salt using a whisk or fork.

8. Once the fritters have cooked, set them on a wire rack and drizzle the glaze over the top. Allow them to rest for 5 minutes so that the glaze sets a little before eating.

Disclaimer

This book contains opinions and ideas of the author and is meant to teach the reader informative and helpful knowledge while due care should be taken by the user in the application of the information provided. The instructions and strategies are possibly not right for every reader and there is no guarantee that they work for everyone. Using this book and implementing the information/recipes therein contained is explicitly your own responsibility and risk. This work with all its contents, does not guarantee correctness, completion, quality or correctness of the provided information. Misinformation or misprints cannot be completely eliminated.

Printed in Great Britain
by Amazon

74897129R00066